Embellished Square Triangle Fold

A three-dimensional embellishment on the front of a square triangle fold card adds visual and textural interest.

Jolie and Jeremy Larson

Paper Casting Designs

Use our inexpensive alternative to cast your own creative dimensional paper designs.

1. Soak tissue in running water and remove the excess water with your fingers.

2. Turn the rubber stamp rubber side up and place tissue on the stamp.

3. Press tissue with a dry towel to remove as much water as possible.

4. Carefully remove the tissue and dry for 24 hours.

Paper Casting

MATERIALS: Plain (no pattern) facial tissue or toilet tissue • Rubber stamp • Towel • Scissors • Radiant Pearls paint • Spray fixative

INSTRUCTIONS: Layer 10 squares of toilet tissue or fold 5 facial tissues in half. Run under water to soak tissue. Using your index and middle fingers, wring as much water as you can out of the tissue. Turn stamp rubber side up and place wet tissue on stamp. With a dry towel, press out as much water as possible. Rotate towel to keep it dry. For a torn edge look, slowly pull excess tissue away from stamp using the wood edge of the stamp for a guide. Carefully lift tissue off the stamp and lay aside to dry for 24 hours. Once the paper cast image is dry, trim edges of paper with plain or decorative scissors. Paint image with Radiant Pearls. Spray with fixative. Glue on card.

Bridesmaid Dress - 7" x 10" piece of *Papers by Catherine* Lime Green cardstock • 4½" x 6½" piece of *Colors by Design* Yellow flower print paper • *Inkadinkado* dress rubber stamp • 4 Lime Green *Stickopotamus* flower photo corners • Bone folder • Glue

INSTRUCTIONS: Follow directions for making paper cast of dress. Paint and trim around edges of the dress. Print, write or stamp information on cardstock. Fold cardstock in center and crease well. Place photo corners on print paper and center on card. Glue dress on the center of the card.

Baby Hand Print - 4" square of *Petals and Papers* Pink mulberry paper • 5½" x 11" piece of *Paper Adventures* Diamond Dust paper • 5" x 11" piece of *Papers by Catherine* Pink vellum • *PSX* baby hand rubber stamp • 14" of ⅛" Pink *Offray* ribbon • Deckle scissors • Bone folder • Glue

INSTRUCTIONS: Follow instructions for making paper cast of hand. Score Diamond Dust paper in the center, fold and crease well. Print, write or stamp information on vellum and trim to 5" x 10". Score in center, fold and crease well. Place vellum inside the card. Make sure the fold is at the top of the card. Hold vellum and card together with ribbon by placing ribbon across inner fold, bringing over the top of the card and tying at the side. Glue paper cast on mulberry paper. With your fingertip, wet edges of the mulberry paper around the paper cast. Gently pull apart creating a torn edge. Glue on the center of the card.

Floral Bridal Shower - *Petals and Papers* (8½" x 11" piece of floral paper, 3¾" x 8½" piece of White cardstock) • *JudiKins* letter rubber stamp • Pressed flower • Deckle scissors • Bone folder • Glue

INSTRUCTIONS: Follow instructions for making paper cast of letter. Trim around paper cast with deckle scissors. Tear one edge of floral paper and fold into thirds with the torn edge at the top. Glue pressed flower on center of torn edge. Print, write or stamp invitation information on cardstock leaving room on the left side for paper cast. Glue paper cast in place, fold card closed.

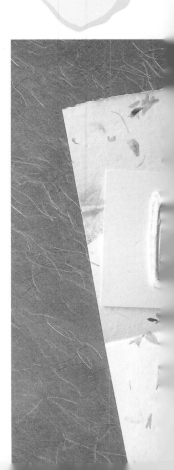

We would be delighted
if you could join us
for afternoon tea in honor
of our future sister-in-law
Nicole Payton
We will shower her with gifts
on July 9th
at 2:00pm
Annie Wiggins Guest House
902 Park Avenue
Galena, Illinois

Shannon Smith
R.s.v.p. 777-6647

Please join us for a
Bridal Shower
honoring

Kristen Anderson

Saturday, July 15th
3:00pm
Kristen's Garden
1826 Story Street
Boone, Iowa

Spinner Invitations

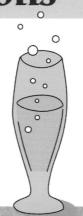

1. Make a tiny hole in the center of the card and circle.

2. Punch a square or circle in the top of the card.

3. Insert brad through holes in the card and circle.

4. Glue the sides of the card together. Do not glue circle.

Spinner Invitations

MATERIALS: 6" x 12" piece of cardstock • 2 colors of cardstock for spinner • Paper brad • Emagination Crafts square or circle punch • Craft knife • Bone folder • Scissors • Ruler • Glue

INSTRUCTIONS: Trace and cut out card and circles using patterns and diagram. With craft knife, make a tiny hole through the center of the card and the circles. Fold and crease card well. Punch a square or circle at the center top of the front panel of the card. Glue circles together. Place the circle in the card and mark areas for adding information. Remove, write information and add embellishments to circle. You should be able to use 3 or 4 pieces of information. Place the circle in the center of the folded card. Punch brad through holes and flatten ends on the back of the card. Glue the sides of the card together leaving the circle free to turn. ●

Spinner Patterns Cut 1 of each. Make center holes in each.

Bridal Shower - *The Paper Cut* cardstock (Green, White, Periwinkle) • *Paper Adventures* Peach cardstock and stickers • Silver heart brad • 1⅝" square punch • Cloud scissors • Glue
INSTRUCTIONS: Follow instructions and make a 5½" square spinner card. Trim the top of front fold with decorative scissors. Cut 5¼" square of Peach cardstock and place inside card. In punched hole, place stickers and write information around circle inside opening. Spin card and add additional information.

Round the Clock Shower - *Paper Adventures* cardstock (Metallic Dark Grey, Metallic White) • 1⅝" square punch • Paper brad • Clock button • 8" of 3" sheer White *Ampelco* ribbon • Hot glue
INSTRUCTIONS: Follow instructions for spinner card. Print or write invitation information on White cardstock and punch out with square punch. Apply glue and place in center of opening on front of card. Spin card and add additional information. Thread ribbon through the back of the clock button and hot glue on the center of the paper brad. Trim ends of ribbon.

It's a Boy! - *Colorbök* (Green dot print, Yellow print, Yellow cardstock) • *The Paper Cut* cardstock (Blue, Purple) • Gold star brad • *Emagination Crafts* 1⅝" and 1⅞" circle punches • Spray adhesive
INSTRUCTIONS: To make 2 sided print paper, spray one side of one piece with spray adhesive, press together and let dry. Follow instructions for spinner card and punch opening with 1⅞" circle punch. Print or write baby information on a piece of Purple cardstock and punch out with 1⅝" circle punch. Apply glue to the back of the circle and place inside opening. Spin the card and add additional information.

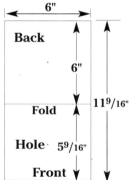

Card Diagram

Follow card dimensions and cut out.

```
         6"
  ←──────────────→
  ┌──────────────┐  ↑       ↑
  │ Back         │  │       │
  │              │  │ 6"    │
  │              │  │       │
  ├ ─ ─ ─ ─ ─ ─ ─┤  ↓       │ 11⁹/₁₆"
  │ Fold         │          │
  │              │  ↑       │
  │ Hole  5⁹/₁₆" │  │       │
  │              │  │       │
  │ Front        │  ↓       ↓
  └──────────────┘
```

An interactive card allows you to spin a wheel to reveal the message.

Poly Shrink Invitations

1. Sand the poly shrink up and down, from side to side.

2. Stamp the image with permanent pigment ink.

It's easy to add any design you desire when you shrink a stamped and colored art image.

3. Color the image with colored pencils or markers.

4. Cut out the image and shrink with an embossing tool or bin an oven.

Poly Shrink Invitations

MATERIALS: Cardstock • Poly Shrink • Rubber stamps • Colored pencils or markers • Ranger permanent pigment ink • Embossing gun or oven • Scissors • 320-400 grit sandpaper • Hot glue

INSTRUCTIONS: Sand the poly shrink up and down and then side to side. Stamp image on poly shrink with permanent pigment ink. Color image with pencils or markers. Cut out image and heat with an embossing tool or bake on medium weight cardboard in regular or toaster oven at 300 to 350°F for approximately 3 minutes. Poly shrink will curl up while being heated and may stick to itself. Allow the pieces to cool then pull apart and reheat the piece to finish shrinking. Use hot glue to attach poly shrink piece to card.

Baby Announcement - *Printworks* assorted pastel print papers • *The Paper Cut* White tri-fold card • 4" x 5" piece of *Papers by Catherine* Metallic Teal cardstock • *Printworks* rubber stamps (lamb, bear, duck) • Black permanent pigment ink • Colored pencils • *Printworks* button and border stickers • *Emagination Crafts* 1 9/16" square punch • Cloud and scallop scissors • Glue
INSTRUCTIONS: Make bear, lamb and duck following poly shrink instructions. Cut off 1/2" from each end of tri-fold card with decorative scissors. Cut 3/4" x 5 1/2" strips of print paper and glue in place. On the inside, run a border sticker down the edge of the paper adhered to the back of each panel to cover line. Add a sticker to bottom. Adhere invitation information to center panel. Punch 3 squares from different papers. Glue lamb, bear and duck on squares. Glue squares on cards referring to photo.

Bride and Groom - 8 1/2" x 11" piece of *Papers by Catherine* Red textured cardstock • 3 1/2" x 5" and 4" x 8 1/2" pieces of *The Paper Cut* White cardstock • *Ducks in a Row* bride and groom rubber stamp • Black permanent pigment ink • 16" of 7/8" sheer Red *Midori* ribbon • Red and Black markers
INSTRUCTIONS: Follow instructions for making poly shrink bride and groom. Score and fold one end of Red cardstock in 2" then score and fold in half. With craft knife, make a small cut in the center of the 2" fold. Slide ribbon through the opening, fold over 2" flap and glue ends down to form pocket. Write invitation on larger piece and reception information on smaller piece of White cardstock. Glue invitation on the inside of the front making sure that the ribbon continues across the card and under the invitation. Insert reception information in 2" pocket. Fold the card in half and tie, trim the ribbon ends. Hot glue bride and groom on the front of the card.

Comfy Space - *The Paper Cut* cardstock (5 1/2" x 11", 3" x 4" and 1" x 3" pieces of White, 4" x 5" piece of Turquoise) • 5" square of *Papers by Catherine* Lavender corrugated paper • *Stampa Rosa* sofa rubber stamp • Black permanent pigment ink • *Emagination Crafts* 1 7/8" circle punch • Blue and Pink markers • Glue
INSTRUCTIONS: Follow instructions for making poly shrink sofa. Score and fold 5 1/2 x 11" cardstock in half. Punch a circle in top corrugated paper. Glue on front of the card. Hot glue poly shrink image in center of opening. On 1" x 3" piece of White cardstock, type or write, 'A comfy space…' and glue on corrugated paper. On remaining White cardstock, add '…in a new place!' and your moving information. Layer Turquoise paper and moving information, glue inside card.

HARPER ROSE LARSON
AND
COOPER ANDREW WILLIAMS

INVITE YOU TO SHARE
IN THE JOY
AS THEY EXCHANGE
MARRIAGE VOWS
ON
SATURDAY THE FIFTH OF
TWO THOUSAND
AT
FIVE O'CLOCK
ST

Creating Wonderfully Fun

Pretty paper sleeves hold pull-out cards. Use them for any occasion… weddings to anniversary celebrations.

1. Cut out the sleeve, fold and crease well.

2. Punch half circle in the end of the sleeve to accommodate the knot on the ribbon.

Rattle & Silver Wedding Sleeve Pattern

Sleeve & Card

MATERIALS: Cardstock • Emagination Crafts 1¼" round and ⅛" hole punches • Ribbon • Bone folder • Scissors • Glue

INSTRUCTIONS: Trace the pattern, cut out the cardstock and score. Cut on solid lines, score on dotted lines. Fold and crease well. Fold sides together and glue in place. Fold up bottom flap and glue in place. Punch a half circle in the open end of the card. Print, stamp or write information on cardstock. Punch a hole at the top of cardstock, thread ribbon and tie a knot. Trim the ends of the ribbon.

3. Glue sleeve seam. Fold up the bottom and glue.

4. Punch 2 holes in the top of the card, thread ribbon through holes and tie a knot.

Rattle Announcement - 7¾" x 11" piece of *Lasting Impressions* Yellow checked cardstock • 4⅞" x 6⅞" piece of *The Paper Cut* White cardstock • 12" of 2" sheer White *Ampelco* ribbon • Rattle button
INSTRUCTIONS: Cut out and follow instructions for rectangle sleeve using Yellow cardstock. Print, stamp or write announcement information on White cardstock. Glue rattle button to top of White cardstock. Slide into sleeve.

Tah Dah! - 8¾" x 9" piece of *Colorbök* Yellow cardstock • *The Paper Cut* cardstock (4" x 9" piece of Mint Green, 3¾" x 8⅞" piece of White) • *Paper Adventures* baby sticker • 12" of 1½" Lavender dot *Offray* ribbon • *Emagination Crafts* 1⁹⁄₁₆" square punch • Cloud scissors
INSTRUCTIONS: Follow instructions for rectangle sleeve using Yellow cardstock. Punch a square as shown on diagram. Fold and glue. Instead of punching half a circle at the open end, trim off ½" with cloud scissors. Print, stamp or write information on White cardstock. Glue cardstock pieces together. Slide cardstock into sleeve. Place baby sticker in the center of the square opening.

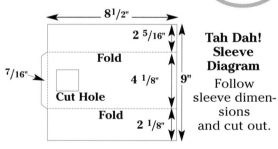

Diagram labels: 8½" • 7/16" • 2 5/16" • **Fold** • 4 1/8" • 9" • **Cut Hole** • **Fold** • 2 1/8"

Tah Dah! Sleeve Diagram Follow sleeve dimensions and cut out.

Silver Wedding - 7¾" x 11" piece of *Paper Adventures* Silver swirl cardstock • *The Paper Cut* cardstock (4⅞" x 6⅞" piece of Silver metallic, 4¾" x 6¾" piece of White) • 12" of 2" sheer White *Ampelco* ribbon • Photo
INSTRUCTIONS: Follow the instructions for rectangle sleeve using Yellow cardstock. Before gluing together, punch a square at the top of the sleeve. Print, stamp or write the announcement information on White cardstock.
TIP: Use a punched out photo or print the photo directly on the cardstock.

Vellum Flower - 6⅛" x 11½" piece of *Frances Meyer* flower vellum • *The Paper Cut* cardstock (5" square of White, 5¼" square of Lavender) • 12" of 2" Lavender *Offray* ribbon
INSTRUCTIONS: Follow instructions for making square sleeve using vellum. Print, stamp or write information on White cardstock. Glue cardstock pieces together. Slide into sleeve.

Vellum Flower Sleeve Pattern

Pull-Out Cards

Envelope Invitations

Elevate the plain envelope to a work of art. Match colors and embellishments to the occasion.

1. Trace and cut out the card. Cut on the solid lines and fold on the dotted lines.

2. Punch 2 holes on flap referring to the diagram.

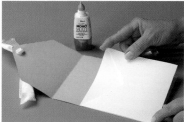

3. Glue the folded pocket to the envelope piece.

4. Decorate the holder with stickers. Attach hook and loop tape for closure. Insert the printed message.

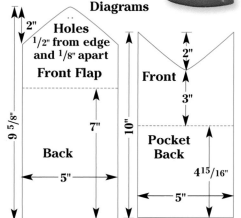

Envelope

MATERIALS: 8½" x 11" pieces of print paper and cardstock • Cardstock for information • Ribbon • Hook and loop tape • ¼" hole punch • Pencil • Decorative scissors • Spray adhesive • Glue

INSTRUCTIONS: If using print paper, attach pieces back to back with spray adhesive before cutting out. Draw and cut out pattern following diagrams. Cut on solid lines, fold on dotted lines. Use decorative scissors to trim straight lines on pattern. Punch holes as indicated on envelope flap, thread ribbon and make an easy bow. Glue pocket on envelope. Print, write or stamp invitation on cardstock and slide in the envelope. Cut a tiny piece of hook and loop tape and attach to the flap and pocket for closure.

Sillybration - *Paper Adventures* (multi color squares print paper, multi color dot, two-tone Blue cardstock, 4½" x 5¾" piece of Yellow cardstock) • 9" of 3" sheer Lavender *Ampelco* ribbon • Party hat button • Zig zag scissors

INSTRUCTIONS: Follow instructions for making envelope. Instead of making an easy bow, bring the ends of the ribbon up through the holes to the front of the flap. Cross the ends through the back of the button. Print, write or stamp information on Yellow cardstock. Slide card into the envelope.

Afternoon Tea Envelope Diagrams

Baby Squares - *Colorbök* print paper (pastel squares, Green dot) • *Paper Adventures* two-tone Yellow cardstock • 4¼" x 5¾" piece of *The Paper Cut* Light Blue cardstock • 9" of 2" sheer Pink *Ampelco* ribbon • Cloud scissors

INSTRUCTIONS: Follow instructions for making envelope. Print, write, or stamp information on Light Blue cardstock. Slide card into envelope.

Afternoon Tea - *Paper Adventures* cardstock (two-tone Pink, two-tone Yellow) • *The Paper Cut* cardstock (3⅝" x 5¾" piece of White, 3¾" x 5⅞" piece of Green) • *Printworks* vellum flower stickers • 9" of 2" sheer flower *Ampelco* ribbon

INSTRUCTIONS: Follow instructions for making envelope. Print, write, or stamp information on White cardstock and glue on Green cardstock. Place stickers on card and envelope. Slide card into envelope.

Sillybration & Baby Squares Envelope Diagrams

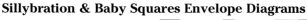

It's a Birthday
Sillybration!
Cooper is Turning Four!
Help us celebrate his special day
at a Birthday-Play Par-tee!
January 14, 2002
at 3:00pm
Cooper's House
604 Bench

Our hearts are full of love for
Morgan Rachel
She came to us
on May 15, 1996
with blue eyes, blonde hair
and skin so very fair
her weight was 8 lb. 13 oz.
her length was 21 inches
Our hearts and home are complete

We would be delighted
if you could join us
for afternoon tea in honor
of our future daughter-in-law
Holly Hook
We will shower her with gifts
on March 30, 2001
at 1:00 pm
Gables & Gardens
and Keeler
Galena, Illinois

Shannon Smith
77-6

Pocketbook Invitations

Ladies will want to add these dainty invitation containers to their collection of sweet treasures.

To make the pocketbook, just cut out, fold and crease, then glue.

Add the handle and embellishments and you are through.

Insert your invitation or use the pocketbook as a gift box to a friend.

These little treasures will no doubt be used again and again!

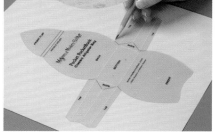

1. Cut out the pocketbook using the template.

2. Fold and crease well.

3. Make the triangle side folds. Fold up as shown.

4. Glue side fold to inside of the pocketbook.

Pocketbook Invitations

MATERIALS: Cardstock or print paper • Museum of Modern Rubber Pocketbook templates • Copy machine • Ribbon or cord • Hook and loop tape • Embellishments • 1/8" hole punch • Scissors • Glue

INSTRUCTIONS: Trace template on cardstock or print paper. Follow instructions that come with the templates. Embellish the flap. Punch hole near top of each side. Slip ends of ribbon through holes and tie knot inside the pocketbook. Print, write or stamp information on White cardstock and trim to fit inside pocketbook. Attach small pieces of hook and loop tape to the flap and front of the pocketbook for the closure.

Baby Shower - 3¼" x 4¼" piece of *The Paper Cut* White cardstock • Scrap in a Snap (Blue cardstock, Yellow check cardstock, Yellow bootie die cut) • Alligator pocketbook template • 36" of ⅛" White satin *Ampelco* ribbon
INSTRUCTIONS: Follow instructions for pocketbook. Trace and cut out a second front flap section from the check paper. Glue the flap sections together. Glue die cut on flap. Cut ribbon into 6 pieces, knot ends together. Print, write or stamp information on White cardstock and trim to 3¼" x 4¼". Slip inside pocketbook.

Spring Shopping Trip - *Scrap in a Snap* cardstock (Blue, Yellow dot print) • *The Paper Cut* White cardstock • *Museum of Modern Rubber* alligator pocket book template • Copper *Artistic* Wire • 4" Orange silk flower • Tape
INSTRUCTIONS: Follow instructions for pocketbook. Trace and cut out a second front flap section from Yellow dot paper. Glue flap sections together. Coil wire around a pencil to make a 6" handle, insert ends in holes and tape to secure. Glue flower on the front of the flap. Print, write or stamp information on White cardstock and trim to 3¼" x 4¼". Slip inside pocketbook.

Let's Get Wild - *The Paper Cut* White cardstock • *NRN Designs* zebra print paper • *Museum of Modern Rubber* tote bag template • 10" of Black feather boa • 6" of 1" Black satin *Offray* ribbon • Hot glue
INSTRUCTIONS: Follow instructions for tote. Instead of placing handle on the front and back of tote, punch holes in the side and knot ends of ribbon inside the tote. Glue boa around top of the tote. Print, write or stamp information on White cardstock and trim to 2¼" x 4½". Slip inside tote.

It's a Baby Shower
Nicole
Arringdale

Beth Garrett's House
1726 Sherry St.
June 15

It's That Time Again
Spring Shopping Trip!
We're meeting at Angela's.
Don't be late, 'cuz we won't wait!

May 14-15

Let's Get Wild!
It's Oliver's last night
of being a single girl

Friday June 3rd
8:00 p.m.

Clever Fold Out Z Cards

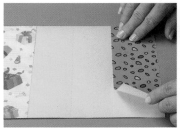

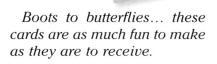

Boots to butterflies… these cards are as much fun to make as they are to receive.

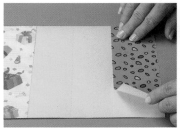 **1.** Glue a print paper to left and right edges of the card.

 **2.** Glue circles evenly spaced across the side of the card.

 **3.** Cut around the circles on the solid paper only.

 **4.** Glue the circles with stickers on the first circles. Fold the card.

Card

MATERIALS: Print paper • Plain paper • Cardstock • Stickers • Scissors • Emagination Crafts 2" circle punch • Ruler • Bone folder • Craft knife • Glue

INSTRUCTIONS: Cut 7¼" x 9¼" piece of cardstock. From the left side score at 2½" and 4¾". Print, write or stamp invitation information along the right side of the 4¾" score line. Fold the first score to the back and second score to the front forming a Z. Crease well and unfold. Cut two 2½" x 7¼" strips of print paper or cardstock. Glue one on the left edge of the card and the other on the right edge. Punch 3 circles from cardstock and embellish with stickers or die cuts. Glue circles down the center of the first fold. Let dry. Cut along the outside right half of the circle with a craft knife. Fold card back into a Z.

Floral Birthday - *K & Company* (pastel stripe print paper, embossed flower paper, butterfly stickers, photo corners) • *The Paper Cut* Metallic White cardstock • *Papers by Catherine* Green cardstock

INSTRUCTIONS: Follow directions for making a card. In addition to punching cardstock circles, punch 3 circles from embossed paper with a flower in the center of each circle. Layer circles and glue together. Add stickers and photo corner as shown in photo.

It's a Boy! - *Colors by Design* pastel stripe print paper • *Papers by Catherine* Yellow cardstock • *The Paper Cut* cardstock (White, 2" x 4½" piece of Light Blue, textured Light Green) • *Paper Adventures* baby stickers • *Emagination Crafts* 1¼" circle punch

INSTRUCTIONS: Follow directions for making a card. Instead of placing information directly on the card, print on Light Blue cardstock and glue along the right side of the second score line. Before placing stickers on 2" Light Blue circles, punch 1¼" Light Green circles. Layer circles and glue together. Add stickers.

Lil' Buckaroo - *NRN Designs* (cow print paper, boot stickers) • *The Paper Cut* White cardstock • *Paper Adventures* Yellow cardstock • Scrap of Red corrugated cardstock • *Emagination Crafts* 2" circle punch

INSTRUCTIONS: Follow directions for making a card.

Embossed Metal Embellishments

Just stamp, trace, emboss and cut the tin or copper to make an unusual embellishment for your card.

To attach your embossed design, glue or use eyelets.

Embossed metal adds a rich gleam to the front of these simple cards.

1. Place a cut piece of metal on a rubber mat and the stamped image on the metal. Trace the image with a fine point stylus.

2. For a debossed look, turn the metal over and retrace the image. Emboss puffy areas with the eraser end of a pencil.

3. Trim the embossed metal with decorative scissors.

Embossing

MATERIALS: Cardstock • Tin or Copper • Rubber stamp • Ink pad • Scrap paper • Fine point stylus • Ruler • Scissors • Glue

INSTRUCTIONS: Stamp design on a piece of scrap paper. Place a cut piece of tin or copper on a soft surface or rubber mat. Place stamped image on top of tin and trace onto metal with stylus. For a puffy embossed design, flip metal over and trace around the lines again. Emboss puffy areas using the eraser end of a pencil to achieve depth. For a debossed look, trace design and then flip tin over. Glue on card.

Diamond Ring Engagement Party - 6" x 12" piece of *Paper Adventures* Metallic Silver cardstock • 2½" x 3½" piece of *ArtEmboss* Tin • *Personal Stamp Exchange* ring rubber stamp • Copy machine

INSTRUCTIONS: Stamp image onto paper and enlarge 130% on a copy machine. Follow instructions for embossed tin. Trim tin to 1½" x 2½". Score cardstock and at 6", fold and crease to make a 6" square card. Print, write or stamp information inside card. Glue tin piece on the center front of the card.

Bride & Groom - *Paper Adventures* cardstock (6" x 9" piece of two-tone Blue, 2½" x 4¼" piece of Peach) • 3" x 4¾" piece of *The Paper Cut* Light Green cardstock • 4" x 9" piece of *Colors by Design* Yellow print paper • 3" x 5" piece of *ArtEmboss* Tin • *Artee Stamps* bride and groom rubber stamp • Deckle scissors

INSTRUCTIONS: Follow directions for debossing tin. Trim tin to 2¼" x 4". Turn cardstock so the darker side is facing up, score 4" from left side. Trim to 5½" x 9" with deckle scissors. Fold and crease well. Print, write or stamp wedding invitation in the center of the 4" section. Glue print paper inside the front flap with the pattern to the outside. Layer tin, Peach cardstock trimmed with deckle scissors and Green cardstock. Glue on the center front of the card.

We've Moved Again - *K & Company* Green (6" x 9" piece of embossed Lime Green paper, corner stickers) • 3½" x 5" piece of *Papers by Catherine* Purple iridescent paper • 4½" x 5" piece of *ArtEmboss* Copper • *Stampa Rosa* house rubber stamp • *Impress Rubber Stamps* (4 Lime Green eyelets, paper punch, setter) • Copy machine

INSTRUCTIONS: Stamp image on paper and enlarge 130% on a copy machine. Follow instructions for puffy embossed design. Trim copper to 3½" x 4". Place copper on left side of cardstock. Punch holes through copper and cardstock. Place eyelet in holes, turn over and set. Print, write or stamp moving information on Purple iridescent paper. Glue on right side of cardstock. Place corner stickers over the corners of Purple paper.

We've moved again
but we haven't traveled far
We're sending you a note
so you'll know where we are!
Andy, Shannon & Cooper
are now residing at
121 Windy Lane
Galena, Illinois
61036

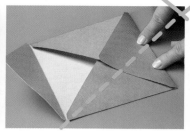

1. Trace the pattern, cut out and score on the dotted lines.

2. Fold the envelope and crease well.

3. Place the invitation inside the envelope.

4. Fold envelope together and tie with a ribbon or seal.

Cut Slits for Ribbon

Baby Shower - *Paper Adventures* ($9\frac{1}{2}$" square of two-tone Blue cardstock, $4\frac{1}{4}$" x $6\frac{1}{4}$" piece and a scrap of Yellow baby print paper, 5" x 7" piece and 2" square of Pink diamond dust paper) • 4" x $5\frac{1}{4}$" piece of *The Paper Cut* vellum • 6" of $\frac{1}{4}$" Yellow satin *Offray* ribbon • *Emagination Crafts* $\frac{1}{8}$" circle punch
INSTRUCTIONS: Follow instructions and make 5" x 7" envelope. Print, write or stamp shower information on vellum. Layer print paper on diamond dust and glue together. Center vellum on print paper and punch 2 holes. Thread the ribbon through the holes and tie an easy bow. Cut an image from the print paper. Glue image on 2" square. Fold envelope. Glue the square to seal the envelope.

Perfume Bottle Invitation - *Paper Adventures* ($9\frac{1}{2}$" square of Green print paper, $9\frac{1}{2}$" square of Yellow perfume bottle print paper, scrap of perfume bottle print paper, 5" x 7" and $4\frac{1}{2}$" x $6\frac{1}{2}$" pieces of two-tone Pink cardstock) • 18" of 3" sheer Lavender *Ampelco* ribbon • Spray adhesive
INSTRUCTIONS: Attach 2 pieces of print paper back to back with spray adhesive. Follow instructions for making 5" x 7" envelope. Print, write or stamp shower information on dark side of $4\frac{1}{2}$" x $6\frac{1}{2}$" piece of two-tone cardstock. Glue on light side of 5" x 7" piece of two-tone cardstock. Cut a perfume bottle from print paper and glue on the top of the invitation. Fold envelope, wrap with ribbon and tie a bow.

Floral Wedding - 5" square of *Petals and Papers* floral paper • 8" square of *Paper Adventures* Green cardstock • $4\frac{3}{4}$" square of *The Paper Cut* vellum • 36" of $1\frac{1}{2}$" sheer Cream *Offray* ribbon • Craft knife
INSTRUCTIONS: Follow instructions for making the square envelope. Cut slits as indicated on pattern. Print, write or stamp information on vellum. Place vellum on floral paper. Thread ribbon through the slits. Place invitation in envelope and fold top, bottom and then the sides of envelope. Tie ribbon in a bow.

Easy Bow - Pull both end of ribbon through the holes on the top of the card. Cross ribbon ends in the back and bring up through the holes on the opposite sides. Trim the ribbon ends.

**Baby Shower & Perfume Bottle
Envelope Pattern**

Cut Slits for Ribbon

Floral Wedding Envelope Pattern

4-Fold Envelope Invitations

Encase your invitations in colorful envelopes that are quick and easy to make.

Envelope
MATERIALS: Patterned paper • Cardstock • Vellum • Ribbon • Scissors • Ruler • Bone folder • Glue
INSTRUCTIONS: Trace pattern. Cut out on solid lines and score on dotted lines. Fold and crease well. Place invitation inside. Fold together and seal or tie with ribbon.

Create a Baby Diaper Announcement

Bottles & booties, diapers & pins, this is where the love begins.

Molly Lane

There expecting a baby, a new bundle of joy,
a very special gift, be it a girl or a boy!

Changing a diaper has never been so much fun. Choose your favorite colors and patterns of paper for these unique announcements and invitations.

Diaper

MATERIALS: Cardstock, Vellum, Handmade paper - just about any kind of paper will work • Ribbon • Pieces of cardstock for information • McGill corner punch • Emagination 1/8" hole punch • Bone folder • Scissors

INSTRUCTIONS: Trace and cut out diaper, cutting on solid lines, scoring on dotted lines. Fold on scores and crease well. Punch 4 holes where indicated by dots. Print, write or stamp information on a piece of cardstock and trim to 4 1/4" x 5 1/4". Round corners with corner punch. Place inside diaper and fold diaper. Thread ribbon through holes and tie a bow.

Pink Polka Dot - *Lasting Impressions* Pink dot cardstock • 4 1/4" x 5 1/4" piece of *The Paper Cut* White linen cardstock • 12" of 3/8" sheer White *Offray* ribbon
INSTRUCTIONS: Follow instructions for diaper. Print, write or stamp information on cardstock. Round corners with punch. Place inside diaper, fold diaper, insert ribbon in holes and tie shut.

Purple Lace - *Petals and Papers* Purple lace paper • 4 1/4" x 5 1/4" piece of *The Paper Cut* vellum • 12" of 1/8" White picot *Offray* ribbon
INSTRUCTIONS: Follow instructions for diaper. Print, write or stamp information on vellum. Round corners with punch. Place inside diaper, fold diaper, insert ribbon in holes and tie shut.

Fold

Hole

● **Hole**

Diaper Pattern

Trace on fold, reverse, trace other half. Include holes on other half.

Fold

Pattern Center Fold (Do not fold card.)

Have you heard the forcast?

A baby is predicted.

But first there will be a shower.

Please join us at a Baby Shower for

Umbrellas - *Papers by Catherine* umbrella vellum • *The Paper Cut* cardstock (4¼" x 5¼" piece of White, 4¼" x 5" piece of Light Green) • 12" of ¼" Light Green picot *Offray* ribbon • Glue
INSTRUCTIONS: Follow instructions for making diaper.

Print, write or stamp information on Light Green cardstock. Round corners with punch. Glue on White cardstock. Place inside diaper, fold diaper, insert ribbon in holes and tie shut.

. Trace and cut out the pattern. Fold and crease well.

2. Punch the holes as indicated on the pattern.

3. Place cardstock inside diaper and fold.

4. Thread the ribbon through the holes and tie a bow.

Spectacular Accordion Invitations

Accordion fold cards look difficult but are a snap to make and the results are simply spectacular!

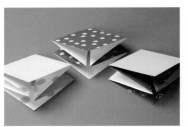

1. Place the 3 squares in vertical order.

Accordion Fold

MATERIALS: Book board or chipboard • Patterned paper • Cardstock • Scissors • Ruler • Bone folder • Spray adhesive • Glue

INSTRUCTIONS: Cut three 8" squares of cardstock or print paper. If using print paper, attach another piece of print paper to back with spray adhesive before cutting. Score 8" squares across center horizontally and vertically making a + on square. Fold and crease well. Turn square over and score square on the diagonal. Fold and crease well. Turn square back over to look like a diamond. There should be 2 folds making an X in the center and one fold in the opposite direction across center. Bring bottom corner of square up to top pushing in sides with fingers and fold into a 4" square. Repeat with remaining 2 squares. Fold one 4" square with print side out. Two 4" squares will have print side in.

Place 3 squares on table in order vertically. Turn center square over. Glue bottom front of first square to top back of second square. Glue bottom back of second square to top front of third square. Fold all 3 squares together making one 4" square.

Cut two 4¼" squares of book board. Cut two 5" square pieces of print paper. Place book board in center. Cut corners of paper at an angle just above corners of book board. Fold sides of paper in and glue. Repeat with second board. Place a strip of glue across inside of one book board and press center of ribbon in glue. Glue back of bottom folded square on inside of book board. Glue back of top folded square on inside of remaining book board. Print, write or stamp party information on scrap pieces of cardstock and trim to 3" squares. Glue 3" squares down center of card. Embellish. Fold card, wrap ribbon around to front and tie shut.

2. Glue the bottom front of the first square to the top back of the second square.

3. Glue the bottom back of the second square to the top front of the third square.

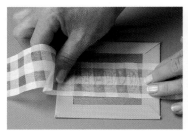

4. Glue the center of the ribbon across the inside of the covered board.

5. Glue the back of the bottom square to the inside of the board.

6. Glue the back of the top square on the inside of the remaining board.

7. Fold accordion, wrap the ribbon to the front and tie to secure booklet.

Baby Announcement - *Colors by Design* print paper (Green dot, Blue dot, Blue and Green) • 4" torn squares of *Hero Arts* Blue and Green Mulberry paper • *The Paper Cut* Metallic White cardstock • 18" of 1½" sheer Cream *Ampelco* ribbon • *EK Success* letter and heart punches
INSTRUCTIONS: Follow instructions for accordion fold. Punch out a B, Y and a heart to spell BOY from the Metallic White cardstock. Glue the letters to a piece of Green mulberry paper and adhere inside top of the accordion card. Glue mulberry paper on inside bottom of card.

Butterfly Birthday - *Paper Adventures* (Green butterfly print paper, Green swirl print paper, two-tone Pink cardstock) • *Jolee's Boutique Stickopotamus* flower photo corners • 18" of 2" sheer variegated *Ampelco* ribbon
INSTRUCTIONS: Follow instructions for accordion invitation. Instead of gluing information squares to the inside of the card, attach them with photo corners. Cut a butterfly out of the print paper, bend the wings up and glue to the front cover of the invitation.

BOY

Cooper
Andrew
Williams

January 14
10:04 pm
7lbs 14oz
21 inches

Proud Parents
Andy & Shannon
Williams

It's a
Birthday
Party!

Rachel's
turning eight,
come & help us
celebrate!

Saturday the
third of June,
one o'clock in
the afternoon!

Third & Vine
is the place to be,
we'll have a blast
just wait and see!

Ribbon Laced Booklet Invitations

Lace your booklets with ribbon... these invitations are sure to be keepers.

1. Glue the embossed paper cards together back to back.

2. Punch 3 to 6 holes evenly down side of cardstock.

3. Punch matching holes down the side of the embossed paper cards.

4. Layer the papers and lace them together with ribbon.

5. Cross the ribbon to the back, lace back up the card.

6. Tie a pretty bow at the end of the card.

Booklet Invitation

MATERIALS: Embossed cardstock or vellum • Colored cardstock • Paper punch • Ribbon • Scissors • Ruler • Glue

INSTRUCTIONS: Cut two 5" x 7" pieces of embossed paper. Cut two 10" x 7" pieces of colored cardstock score in the center, fold and crease well to make two 5" x 7" cards. Print, write or stamp information on the inside of the cards. Glue the 5" x 7" cards together, back to back. Place the 2 embossed pieces on top and bottom. Punch 3 to 6 holes down the folded side of the cards. You may have to punch pieces separately and then align holes to punch layers. Tie ribbons in holes to hold together or lace down and up the card. To lace the card, start from the back and come up through the first hole with ribbon. Cross to back and come up second hole from the back. Continue down card. Repeat method coming up and pulling ribbon through from the back of the card. Tie the ends together at the top.

90th Birthday Party - *K & Company* (embossed floral vellum, floral and border stickers) • *Strathmore* White water color paper • 36" of ½" sheer Green *Offray* ribbon
TIP: Tear the edges of the watercolor paper.

Alphabet Announcement - *K & Company* embossed alphabet cardstock • *The Paper Cut* Lavender cardstock • 36" of ⅛" Pink satin *Offray* ribbon
TIP: Cut letters from the embossed cardstock.

Birthday Party - *K & Company* embossed toy cardstock • *The Paper Cut* Blue cardstock • 18" of ⅝" sheer Red *Ampelco* ribbon
TIP: Cut toys from the embossed cardstock.

Whose eyes sparkle like the stars?
Whose smile outshines the sun?
Whose skin is soft as moon-glow?
Our precious little one.

Jack-in-the-box stretches his neck to see
the truck toots his horn with glee;
the top twirls around with joy,
in honor of the birthday boy!

COOPER

is turning four years old!
You're invited to a birthday party!
Hope you can come and
clown around with us!

Our hearts are full of love for

EMMA
GRACE

She came to us on
June 3, 2002
with blue eyes, brown hair,
and skin so fair.

Her weight was 7lbs, 14oz,
her length was 21 inches.
Our hearts and home are now complete!

Please join us
Saturday
January 12, 2002
4:00pm

Saturday

January 14

2002

3:00-5:00pm

Punched
Letter Cards

Make titles the easy way with punched letters and shapes to create marvelous cards.

1. Punch letters across the bottom of the card.

2. Stack the papers and punch the holes for ribbon at the top of the card.

Punched Cards

MATERIALS: Cardstock • EK Success letter punches • Bone folder • Scissors • Ruler • Glue

Gabby - 5" x 7" and 4¾" x 6¾" pieces of *Paper Adventures* two-tone Peach cardstock • 4¼" x 5½" piece of *The Paper Cut* vellum • *EK Success* upper case letter punches to spell baby's name • 18" of 3" pearl edge Cream *Ampelco* ribbon • *Emagination Crafts* ⅛" circle punch
INSTRUCTIONS: Use dark side of 5" x 7" and light side of 4¾" x 6¾" cardstock. Punch Gabby across the bottom of the light cardstock. Print or write name meaning and information on vellum. Layer all 3 papers and punch 2 holes in the center top. Thread ribbon through holes and tie a bow.

Easy Bow - Pull both ends of ribbon through the holes on the top of the card. Cross ribbon ends in the back and bring up through the holes on the opposite sides. Trim edges.

Baby Girl - *Papers by Catherine* (Pink accordion card, White Pearl paper) • *EK Success* upper case letter punches to spell GIRL • 18" of 2" sheer Pink *Ampelco* ribbon • *Kolo* White Pearl photo corners • 2 baby photos
INSTRUCTIONS: Trim baby photos to 3" squares. Attach to the first and the last panels of the card with photo corners. Punch the word girl in the remaining inside panels, one letter per panel. Print or write baby information on pearl paper, trim and glue on the top center of each panel. Fold card, wrap with ribbon and tie bow on front of the card.

B is for Baby - *The Paper Cut* cardstock (5½" x 11" and 3" x 4¾" pieces of Metallic White, 4 pastels, 3¼" x 5" piece of Dark Pink) • *EK Success* lower case letter punches to spell baby • *Kolo* Yellow photo corners
INSTRUCTIONS: Score Metallic White cardstock in center, fold and crease well to make a 5½" square card. Print or write the following randomly on the front of the card.

Is for baby - so innocent and sweet.
Is for adorable - bubbly smiles, tiny feet
Is for beautiful - perfect in every way.
Is for yeah - our baby arrived this day!

Punch letters to spell baby from pastel cardstock. Glue on the front of the card next to appropriate line. Print or write information on 3" x 4¾" Metallic White cardstock. Glue on Dark Pink cardstock and attach inside the card using the photo corners.

Inside of **B is for Baby** card.

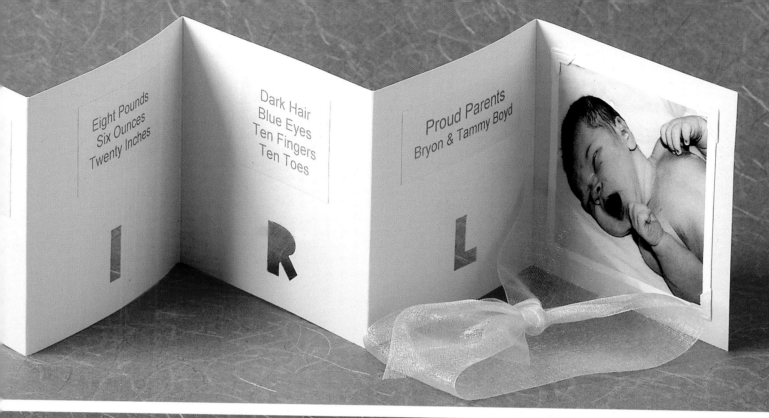

Eight Pounds
Six Ounces
Twenty Inches

Dark Hair
Blue Eyes
Ten Fingers
Ten Toes

Proud Parents
Bryon & Tammy Boyd

Gabby

coming from Gabrielle

Meaning

God is my Strength

May 19th
10:04pm
7lbs 14oz
20inches

GABBY

b *is for Baby – so innocent and sweet.*

a *is for Adorable – bubbly smiles, tiny feet.*

b *is for Beautiful – perfect in every way.*

y *is for Yeah – our baby arrived this day!*

Clay Mold Embellishments

Molded clay shapes add an exquisite finishing touch to vellum and cardstock cards.

1. Roll the clay in your hand to soften and condition.

2. Press clay into the mold making sure to fill all areas.

3. Carefully remove the clay from the mold.

4. Trim the clay, bake, cool and glue on the card.

Clay Molds

MATERIALS: Cardstock • Vellum • Polymer clay • Push mold • Scissors • Ruler • Glue • Hot glue

INSTRUCTIONS: Roll clay in hands until soft. Press into mold making sure to get clay into all areas of the mold. Remove from mold. Following manufacturer's instructions, bake clay. Attach to invitation with hot glue.

Surprise! Surprise! - 6" x 9" piece of *The Paper Cut* Lime Green cardstock • 5½" x 8½" piece of *Colors by Design* Blue and Green squares print paper • 5" x 7" piece of *Papers by Catherine* vellum • Lime Green polymer clay • *Sculpey* Swag Decor push mold
INSTRUCTIONS: Follow instructions for molding and baking clay. Glue print paper on cardstock. Print, write or stamp party information on vellum and place in center of print paper and glue top corners. Hot glue clay on corners.

Purple Medallion - 7" x 10" piece of *Papers by Catherine* White cardstock • 1½" x 11" strip of *Colors By Design* Lavender dot print paper • 3" square of *Colorbök* Pink paper • 5" x 7" piece of *The Paper Cut* Lavender cardstock • Lavender polymer clay • *Sculpey* Swag Decor push mold • *Emagination Crafts* 1⅝" square punch • Bone folder
INSTRUCTIONS: Follow instructions for molding and baking clay. Score lengthwise 2½" in from both ends. Fold and crease well. Print, write or stamp information on Lavender cardstock. Place in the center of the White card and fold sides in. Wrap print paper strip around the card and glue ends together on the back. Punch a square of Pink paper and turn to a diamond shape. Hot glue clay medallion on the center of the diamond. Glue diamond to the center of the strip on the front of the card. To open the card, slip off the band, break the seal on the back or slide the invitation out of the top of the card.

Summer Sun - 5" square of *Paper Adventures* Gold/Pink plaid paper • 4" square of *The Paper Cut* vellum • 6" square of Gold corrugated paper • Magenta polymer clay • *Sculpey* Swag Deco push mold
INSTRUCTIONS: Follow instructions for molding and baking clay. Print, write or stamp party information on vellum. Glue print paper on corrugated paper. Attach vellum to print paper at corners. Hot glue clay on corners of vellum.

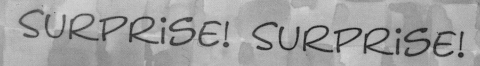

SURPRISE! SURPRISE!

HELP US CELEBRATE

ANDY'S BIRTHDAY

ON DECEMBER 18TH
COCKTAILS - 5:00PM
DINNER - 6:00PM
THE GRAPE ESCAPE
GALENA, ILLINOIS

Summer sun,
girlfriends and fun;
Stay up all night
'till dawn's morning light.

Hannah Boyd
will turn eight years old
on August 22
so she's having a
Slumber Party
The fun starts at
621 Tama Street

Fun & Easy Marbled Paper

Can't find just the perfect paper? Marble your own using this easy technique.

1. Fill cookie sheet with a ¼" thick layer of shaving cream.

2. Drop the ink on the shaving cream in various spots.

3. Swirl the ink in the shaving cream with stick or finger.

4. Place a sheet of paper flat on the shaving cream and press down.

5. Pull the paper up, scrape off excess shaving cream.

6. Wipe the paper clean with a paper towel.

Marbling

MATERIALS: Cardstock • *Inkabilities* ink • Shaving cream • Cookie sheet • Paper towel • Craft stick

INSTRUCTIONS: Fill a cookie sheet with shaving cream approximately ¼" thick. Drop ink into shaving cream in various spots. Using your finger or craft stick, swirl ink around in shaving cream. Place paper flat on shaving cream and press down making sure that all parts of the paper are in the cream. Pull out and scrape off excess shaving cream and wipe clean with a paper towel. Set aside to dry.

Summer Dinner Party - *The Paper Cut* (5" x 7" piece of Neon Orange cardstock, 4½" x 6½" piece of Neon Pink cardstock, 7" x 10" piece of vellum) • *Posh Impressions* Coral & Sunshine Inkabilities • 18" of 1½" Yellow satin *Ampelco* ribbon • Bone folder
INSTRUCTIONS: Follow instructions for marbling cardstock. Print, stamp or write information on marbled paper. Score the vellum 2½" from each end. Fold and crease well. Place invitation in center of vellum, fold shut. Tie ribbon around the invitation.

Blast from the Past - 5" x 7" piece of *The Paper Cut* White cardstock • 4½" x 6½" piece of *EK Success* Lime Green dot vellum • *Posh Impressions* Kiwi & Coral Inkabilities • 2 Silver paper brads
INSTRUCTIONS: Follow instructions for marbling cardstock. Print, stamp or write information on marbled paper. Center the vellum on the marbled paper, punch paper brads through the corners and flatten ends on back.

Bridal Tea - *The Paper Cut* cardstock (5½" x 7½" piece of Sage Green, 4" x 6" piece of White) • 5" x 7" piece of *Paper Adventures* Metallic Purple swirl paper • *Posh Impressions* Eggplant Inkabilities • *K & Company* flower and corner stickers
INSTRUCTIONS: Follow instructions for marbling cardstock. Print, stamp or write information on marbled cardstock. Layer and glue papers together. Apply stickers to the front of the invitation.

Summer is here...
So let's beat the heat
with a refreshing twist!

Please join us for a
Dinner Party

July 5th
Andy & Shannon
Williams'
604 S. Bench

Andy's appetizers and
Shannon's secret drink recipes
are guaranteed to make you
forget all about the heat!

Blast from the Past!

50's were a simple time . . .

box tune cost only a dime

a '57 Chevy was really cool!

Shoppe was the place after school

Let's Rock Around the Clock

on March 8th at 5:00pm

Eagle Ridge Inn & Resort
Galena, Illinois

We would be delighted
if you could join us
for afternoon tea in honor
of our future sister-in-law
Nicole Payton
We will shower her with gifts
on Saturday, March 30th
at 1:00pm
Gables & Garden Tea Room
Boone, Iowa

Angie and Courtney
Arringdale

Winter is depressing us—
so we're planning a

Tropical Escape Party
(if only for an evening)

at Andy & Shannon's
604 S. Bench
January 10th

Tropical drinks served at
5:00pm
and dinner will be served
6:00pm

harper rose larson

and

cooper andrew williams

together with

their parents

Life is a garden
and love is in bloom!
The bridesmaids of
Nicole Payton
invite you to join them
in showering the bride-to-be
at Reiman Gardens
on May 15th
at 2:00pm
1407 Elwood Drive
Ames, Iowa

Please bring a favorite flower
and a gift with a garden theme.

RSVP
Angela Carswell

You are

American

A special evening
Cocktails, Music, Dinner, Dancing
on July 4th
at 5:00pm
Eagle Ridge Inn
Galen